D1084832

THE BEST
CATS
EVER

Siamese ARE THE BEST!

Elaine Landau

LERNER PUBLICATIONS COMPANY · MINNEAPOLIS

Copyright © 2011 by Lerner Publishing Group, Inc.

All rights reserved. International copyright secured. No part of this book
may be reproduced, stored in a retrieval system, or transmitted in any
form or by any means—electronic, mechanical, photocopying, recording, or
otherwise—without the prior written permission of Lerner Publishing Group,
Inc., except for the inclusion of brief quotations in an acknowledged review.

Lerner Publications Company
A division of Lerner Publishing Group, Inc.
241 First Avenue North
Minneapolis, MN 55401 U.S.A.

Website address: www.lernerbooks.com

Library of Congress Cataloging-in-Publication Data

Landau, Elaine.
        Siamese are the best! / by Elaine Landau.
          p.   cm. — (The best cats ever)
        Includes index.
        ISBN 978-0-7613-6427-6 (lib. bdg. : alk. paper)
        1. Siamese cat—Juvenile literature. I. Title.
        SF449.S5L356 2011
        636.8′25—dc22   2010027979

Manufactured in the United States of America
1 — CG — 12/31/10

TABLE OF CONTENTS

LOVELY TO LOOK AT

I'm thinking of a special cat. It has sky blue eyes, a sleek body, and a graceful walk. Can you guess what cat I'm thinking of? It's a **Siamese!**

Siamese cats are lovely to look at. Their legs are slim, and their tails are long. Their heads are a pretty wedge shape. Their ears are large and pointed.

A GREAT NAME FOR A GREAT CAT

A Siamese cat is a terrific pet. Give it a special name. Do any of these names fit your super Siamese?

Bangkok

Jewel

Gracie

Mia

Kasem

Kashmir

Topaz

Sapphire

Siam

Yum-Yum

Siamese are known for their unusual coats. Their coats have a colorpoint pattern. This means their coats are darker on or near the cats' ears, faces, legs, and tails. The darker areas are called points.

A blue point Siamese

Colors of a Cool Cat's Coat

Siamese coats come in different colors. Their coats may be any of these four colors:

- seal point (a tan body with dark brown points)

- chocolate point (a white body with milk chocolate-colored points)

- blue point (a grayish white body with gray points)

- lilac point (a white body with pinkish gray points)

All the coat colors are beautiful. Do you have a favorite?

A lilac point
Siamese

A chocolate point
Siamese

As Round as an Apple

Not all Siamese cats are long and lean. There's another type of Siamese as well. These cats have bigger, rounder bodies. They also have rounder heads and smaller ears. They are known as traditional Siamese cats, or appleheads (*pictured right*). Appleheads make great pets. But you won't often see them competing in cat shows. In the show ring, the slim Siamese is the winner.

Great Purr-sonality

Siamese cats make wonderful pals. They enjoy being around people. These cats often follow their owners around the house. They also like to play with their families. Many Siamese even learn to play fetch!

Siamese cats are super loving. They are quite smart too. Their owners think they have the best cats ever. Can you blame them?

SIAMESE CATS ON THE BIG SCREEN

Have you seen the Disney movie *Lady and the Tramp*? The film's stars are dogs. But the movie also features two Siamese cats named Si and Am *(right)*. You can find Siamese cats in other movies too.

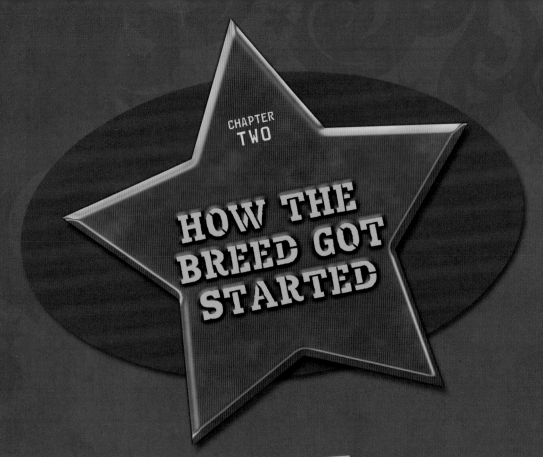

CHAPTER
TWO

HOW THE BREED GOT STARTED

The ruins of Siam's capital city, Ayutthaya

The Siamese is one of the world's oldest cat breeds. It comes from Thailand. That country used to be called Siam. Siamese cats were named for Siam.

A modern-day painting shows what Siamese temple cats may have looked like.

Could It Be True?

Some say that years ago, only Thailand's royals owned Siamese cats. When a royal owner died, the person's cat was taken to a temple.

At the temple, the cat would live in luxury. It would eat only the finest foods. It would sleep on silk pillows. Monks and priests would wait on it.

Why were temple cats treated so well? It's said that Thailand's people thought the cats had special powers. They were thought to protect the souls of their dead owners.

This cat sculpture decorates a temple in Bangkok, Thailand.

COMMERCIAL CATS

Over the years, Siamese cats have been used to sell things. They have been in TV commercials for cat food. They've been spotted in magazine ads too. Siamese cats have even been on postage stamps in several countries.

POSTES LAO 1995

CHATS DE RACE

50K

In 1950, the king of Thailand and his future wife posed for this photo with a Siamese cat.

No one knows for sure if the stories about temple cats are true. But they've been told in Thailand for many years. The tales have become an important part of the country's history and culture.

Out of Thailand

As beloved as Siamese cats were in Thailand, they may have been even more popular in Britain. In the late 1800s, someone brought some Siamese cats to Britain. Before long, these fancy felines started winning top honors in cat shows. People kept the cats as pets too.

A five-week-old Siamese kitten sits in a trophy cup at a London cat show in 1957.

A pet Siamese in Britain laps milk from a bottle in this 1960s photo.

Soon Siamese were taken to the United States. Siamese cats were most popular in the United States during the 1950s. That was when this breed really captured the nation's attention.

These days, people still love Siamese cats. They are among the fifteen most popular cat breeds.

A champion Siamese show cat watches over her litter of kittens in Newton, Massachusetts.

A FIRST DAUGHTERS' FAVORITE

Amy Carter (top) and Susan Ford (bottom) have two things in common. Both are the daughters of former U.S. presidents. And both had Siamese cats. Susan's cat was named Shan Shein. Amy's cat was called Misty Malarky Ying Yang.

IS A SIAMESE YOUR KIND OF CAT?

"I'll take a Siamese, please." That's what you might say after spending time with one of these kitties. After all, Siamese cats have both brains and beauty. That's hard to beat.

But wait! Think before you bring a Siamese into your home. Read on to see if this breed is really right for you.

Busy, Noisy Cats

Do you want a quiet, laid-back kitty? Then you don't want a Siamese. These cats are active and curious. They also "talk" a lot.

A Siamese cat's meow sounds like a baby's cry. At times, it can be even louder. Some people like having a chatty kitty. It drives others crazy. How do you feel about it?

Are you ready for a talkative Siamese?

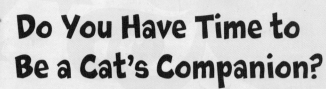

Do You Have Time to Be a Cat's Companion?

Siamese cats become very attached to their owners. They don't like being left alone for very long. Do you have a lot of after-school activities? Are you away from home a lot? Then think twice about getting a Siamese.

AN INDOOR PUSSYCAT

It's important to keep your cat indoors for safety reasons. Outdoors, cats can be hurt by other animals or eat things that might make them sick.

Fortunately, it's not hard to keep most Siamese indoors. These cats love lounging around the house. One of their favorite things to do is to nap in a warm spot. Finding a sunny windowsill is like winning the lottery to them.

A Costly Kitty

Are the best things in life always free? Some people think Siamese are one of the best things—but they definitely aren't free.

Many breeders charge between $650 and $850 for a Siamese kitten. Some charge even more. Can your family afford a pricey pet? Think about this before you fall for a Siamese.

RESCUE A SIAMESE CAT

Not sure you can afford a Siamese kitten? How about getting an older cat? Many older Siamese are available at rescue centers for this breed. Often you can get one for a small fee.

Just remember: All cats are expensive. Even if you adopt a cat from a rescue center or a shelter, your family still will need to pay for food, health care, and pet supplies.

A group of Siamese kitties plays on the stairs.

Have you decided if a Siamese cat is right for you? If it is, you're in for a treat. Few kitties can beat these fine felines when it comes to looks, personality, and charm.

21

HELLO, PRETTY KITTY!

The big day is here at last. It just might be the best day of your life. You're picking up your Siamese cat!

Be Sure You're Ready

Make your cat feel right at home. Have the supplies you'll need. Buy the items below before you pick up your new pet.

- food and water bowls

- cat food

- litter box

- kitty litter

- brush and wide-tooth steel comb

- scratching post

- cat carrier

See a Vet Soon

Don't wait too long to take your cat to a
veterinarian. That's a doctor who treats
animals. They're called vets for short.

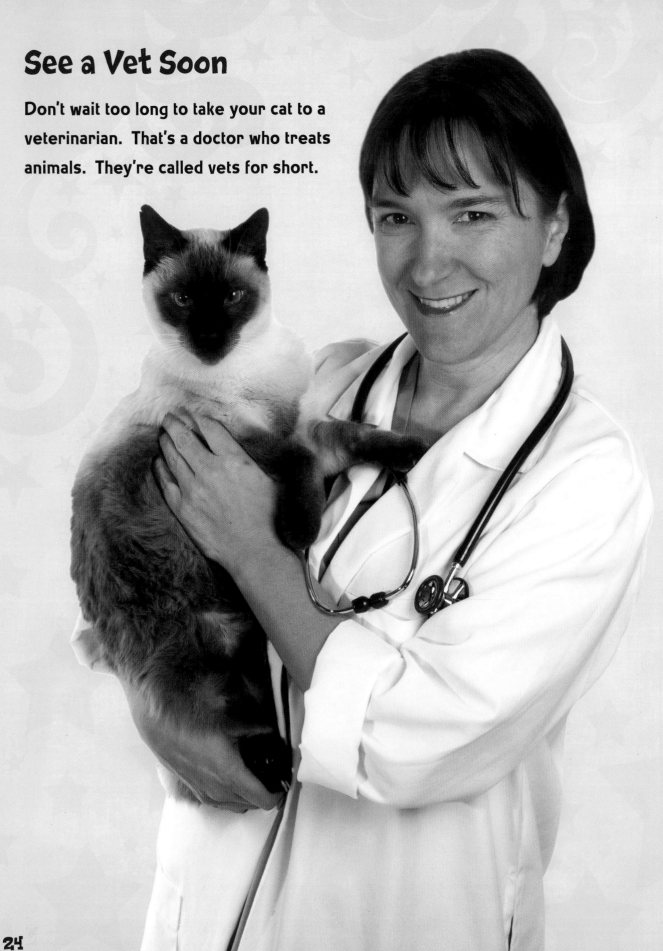

The vet will check your cat's health. Your cat will also get the shots it needs. Take your kitty back to the vet for regular checkups. Also take your cat to the vet if it gets sick.

Take your cat to the vet to make sure he or she stays healthy.

IT'S OK TO PLAY ALL DAY...
IF YOU'RE A SIAMESE CAT

Siamese cats love to play. You can find lots of cat toys at pet shops. Spend some time each day playing with your cat. Don't let your Siamese become bored. Bored Siamese can easily get into trouble.

Feeding Your Furry Friend

Ask your vet what to feed your cat. A cat needs different food at different times in its life. Don't give your cat table scraps. This can lead to an unhealthful weight gain. Remember that you are feeding a slender cat—not a small hippo!

24/7

Your cat should always have cool, clean drinking water—twenty-four hours a day and seven days a week. Water is as important as food. Change your cat's water twice a day.

Good Grooming

Lucky you! Siamese cats don't need a lot of grooming. Brush your cat once a week in the spring. Siamese tend to shed a bit more then, and brushing removes the loose fur. Brushing is needed less often the rest of the year.

Siamese cats don't shed much, but many enjoy a good brushing.

You and Your Siamese

A Siamese cat is not just a cat. It's more like a best buddy. It will always be there for you.

Be sure you are there for it as well. You'll have a special bond with a very special cat. It doesn't get any better than that!

GLOSSARY

applehead: a type of Siamese cat that has a round head and body and small ears. Appleheads are also known as traditional Siamese.

breed: a particular type of cat. Cats of the same breed have the same body shape and general features.

breeder: someone who mates cats to produce a particular type of cat

coat: a cat's fur

colorpoint: a coat pattern in which some parts of a cat's coat are darker than others. The darker areas are on or near the cat's ears, face, legs, and tail.

feline: a cat, or having to do with cats

groom: to clean, brush, and trim a cat's coat

rescue center: a shelter where stray and abandoned cats are kept until they are adopted

shed: to lose fur

veterinarian: a doctor who treats animals. Veterinarians are called vets for short.

FOR MORE INFORMATION

Books

Brecke, Nicole, and Patricia M. Stockland. *Cats You Can Draw*. Minneapolis: Millbrook Press, 2010. Perfect for cat lovers, this colorful book teaches readers how to draw many popular cat breeds, including the Siamese.

Brown, Ruth. *Gracie the Lighthouse Cat*. London: Andersen Press, 2011. Gracie the lighthouse cat and Grace Darling, the lighthouse keeper's daughter, both have an adventure one very windy night.

Hanson, Anders. *Sleek Siamese*. Edina, MN: Abdo, 2010. This book provides information on buying and living with a Siamese cat.

Harris, Trudy. *Tally Cat Keeps Track*. Minneapolis: Millbrook Press, 2011. Tally McNally is a cat who loves to tally—but one day, he gets into a jam. Will his friends find a way to help him?

Landau, Elaine. *Your Pet Cat*. Rev. ed. New York: Children's Press, 2007. This title is a good guide for young people on choosing and caring for a cat.

Stone, Lynn M. *Siamese Cats*. Vero Beach, FL: Rourke, 2010. Stone tells all about Siamese cats in this interesting introduction to the breed.

Websites

ASPCA Kids
http://www.aspca.org/aspcakids
Check out this website for helpful hints on caring for a cat and other pets.

For Kids: About Cats
http://kids.cfa.org
Be sure to visit this website on cats and cat shows. Don't miss the link to some fun games as well.

LERNER e SOURCE™

Expand learning beyond the printed book. Download free, complementary educational resources for this book from our website, www.lerneresource.com.

Index

Photo Acknowledgments

The images in this book are used with the permission of: backgrounds © iStockphoto.com/ javarman3 and © iStockphoto.com/Julie Fisher; © iStockphoto.com/Michael Balderas, p. 1; © Juniors Bildarchiv/Alamy, p. 4 (left); © iStockphoto.com/ Nancy Louie, pp. 4-5; © Ilknur Okan Erdir/ Dreamstime.com, p. 5 (right); © Jane Burton/Dorling Kindersley/Getty Images, p. 6; © jon le-bon/ Shutterstock Images, pp. 6-7; © Philip Dickson/Dreamstime.com, p. 7 (top); © Vitalij Schaefer/ Dreamstime.com, p. 7 (bottom right); © Brenda Carson/Shutterstock Images, p. 8 (top); © Isabella Perez/Photononstop/Photolibrary, p. 8 (bottom); © Richard Hutchings/Digital Light Source/ Photolibrary, p. 9 (top); GTV Archive/Rex Features USA, p. 9 (bottom); The Art Achive/Gianni Dagli Orti, p. 10; Siamese, Freestone, Joan (Contemporary Artist) /Private Collection/The Bridgeman Art Library, p. 11; © Tusia/Shutterstock Images, p. 12 (top); © Steve Mann/Shutterstock Images, p. 12 (bottom); © Picture Post/Hulton Archive/Getty Images, p. 13 (top); © Fotosearch Value/Photolibrary, p. 13 (bottom); © Hulton-Deutsch Collection/CORBIS, p. 14 (top); © Mary Evans Picture Library/ The Image Works, p. 14 (bottom); The Art Archive/Willard Culver/NGS Image Collection, p. 15 (top); Courtesy of Jimmy Carter Library, p. 15 (center right); Courtesy of Gerald R. Ford Library, p. 15 (bottom right); ©Lisovskaya Natalia/Shutterstock Images, p. 16 (left); © David Zanzinger/Alamy, p. 16 (right); © Bob Daemmrich/The Image Works, p. 17; © istockphoto.com/Wladimir Tolstich, p. 18; © Zave Smith/Workbook Stock/Getty Images, p. 19 (top); © J. Silver/SuperStock, p. 19 (bottom); © NaturePL/SuperStock, p. 20; © J-L Klein & M-L Hubert/Bios/Photolibrary, p. 21 (bottom); © Steve Taylor/Stone/Getty Images, p. 21 (top); © Juniors Bildarchive/Photolibrary, p. 22; © Mark Bond/ Dreamstime.com, p. 23 (food); © Eti Swinford/Dreamstime.com, p. 23 (litter box); © iStockphoto. com/Jennifer Sheets, p. 23 (scratching post); © Agita Leimane/Dreamstime.com, p. 23 (brush); © iStockphoto.com/ Joe Belanger, p. 24; © iStockphoto.com/Jose Manuel Gelpi Diaz, p. 25 (top left);© Arco Images/Reinhard H./Alamy, p. 25 (top right); © iStockphoto.com/Suzannah Skelton, p. 25 (bottom); © G.K. Hart/Vikki Hart/White/Photolibrary, p. 26; © Emma Ward/Alamy, p. 27 (top); © Gaertner/Alamy, p. 27 (center); © Kike Calvo VW Pics/SuperStock, p. 27 (bottom); © Gary Randall/ kimballstock.com, p. 28 (top); © Dana Neely/Photodisc/Getty Images, p. 28 (bottom); © Fat Cat Photography/Alamy, p. 29.

Front cover: © iStockphoto.com/Vasiliy Koval.
Back cover: © Juniors Bildarchiv/Alamy.